"Hello? It's Autumn Falling…"

Liz Rumble

BookLeaf Publishing

India | USA | UK

Presentation by *BookLeaf Publishing*

Web: www.bookleafpub.com

E-mail: info@bookleafpub.com

ISBN: 9789358737226

First edition 2023

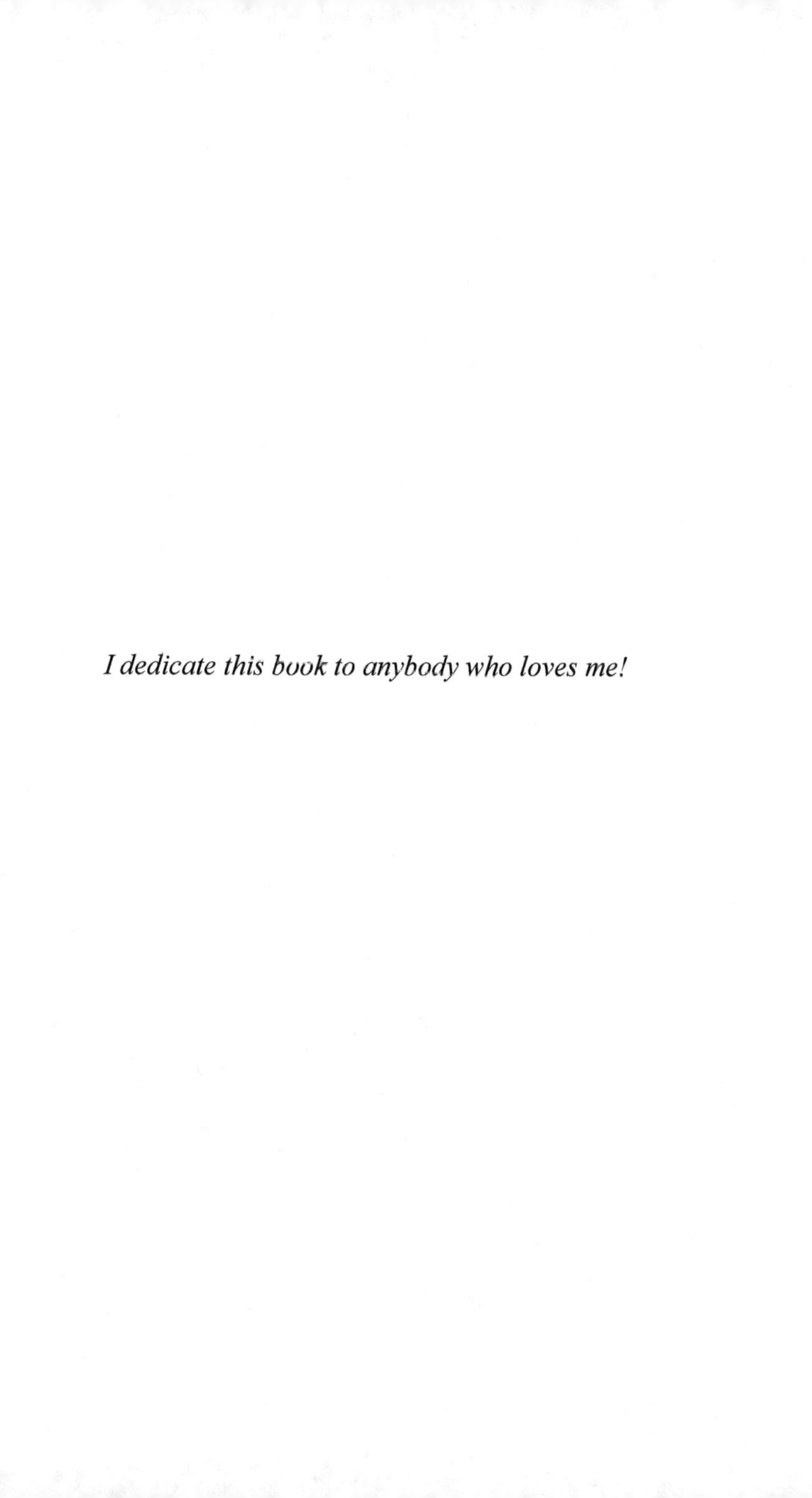

I dedicate this book to anybody who loves me!

ACKNOWLEDGEMENT

Goodness – I've never written acknowledgements before but I totally acknowledge anyone who told me I could do this and anyone who keeps me sane. You know who you are!

PREFACE

Autumn is a funny season. I'm always more pensive in these months. Summer is well and truly over and it's that interesting time between the memories of the sunny, warmer time and the promise of the end of the year. The nights are darker, it gets colder so it makes me want to stay in more; and staying in more means more thinking time.

So these poems are a complete mish-mash of my Autumnal thoughts. You'll see a little explanatory note from me at the end of each poem.

I hope you enjoy! And if you don't, hugest apologies!

Staying in is absolutely the new going out

It's starting to get darker now
The lights are on by six
The dark and dismal season
Is up to its old tricks

I got an invite to the pub
A catch-up and quick drink
But staying in's the new going out
So box sets instead I think!

A trip to town, a little mooch
I admit that sounds quite fun
But I really mustn't venture out
Till jobs and chores are done

New exercise class starts tonight
Sounds good; I've got the gear
But it's quite 'in' to stay in these days
And the sofa would miss my rear!

Count me in; I'll be there!
A gathering sounds brill
But no – atchoo – I'm germ-ridden
And I daren't make you all ill

Couch to 5K sounds doable
But hold on just a min
I'm sure my TV's 4K itself
So I may as well stay in!

I'm definitely going out tonight
(Gasp) Was that a drop of rain?
Or one lone blowing leaf out there?
I can't risk this hurricane!

I promise I will come out soon
There truly is no doubt
But to guarantee I make it there
You'll have to drag me out!

It gets colder, and darker, and I just don't want
to be anywhere but inside my warm, cosy home.
Does anyone else relate?!

A good deed

You see that person next to you?
You have no idea what it is that they do

Builder, director, DJ, nurse
Or an accomplished poet penning their verse

You see that person in front of you?
You have no idea what they're going through

It could be a good thing, it could be bad
Their lives could be happy, or immeasurably sad

You see that person opposite you?
Most likely they are looking at you too

Reciprocally wondering about your life
Its ups and downs, its joy and strife

You see that person sitting behind you?
Probably not – you're obscuring their view!

They may want to pass the time of day
But feel too awkward; what to say?

You see those people all around you?
They've all been on a journey or two

Whether in front or behind; across the aisle
Do a good deed and simply smile.

I enjoy people-watching. Nobody knows what is
going on in somebody's life. A smile can change
someone's day. My favourite quote of all time is
'be kinder than necessary for everyone is
fighting their own battle'.

Surprise, Surprise …

I like nice surprises
The best ones you can get
Are ones that come out of the blue
The ones you least expect

I'm good with surprises
I've given quite a few
I've put a smile on many-a-face
Or at least attempted to

I loathe bad surprises
My heart stops in its track
They make you sad and wish so hard
You could turn the clock back

Surprises do surprise me
Whether big or small
Yet the main surprise I seem to get
Is no surprise at all

I do like a surprise now and again (if it's a nice
one). More often than not, I'm the surpriser
rather than the surprisee. I am surprised if there
are no surprises but equally surprised if there
are!

You and me

Mr Illogical
Miss Common Sense
You are intelligent
But I'm a bit dense
You know about history
I know about shops
You're worldly-wise
I'm totally not
You eat what you want
Food sticks to my hips
I know what to wear
But you need some tips
You understand films
I lose the plot
You're rarely cold
I'm rarely hot
I like to organise
You do not plan
I'm such a woman
You're such a man

* Disclaimer: This is not meant to sum up every
relationship – just mine!

Think before you post

Your comment
Doesn't warrant an answer

Your remark
Has darkened my day

Your retort
Before thought has destroyed me

I sit here
Unsure what to say.

Aimed at the keyboard warriors of today. It is so
easy for somebody to write a hurtful comment
on social media without realising the potential
impact. This is a short, intentionally abrupt,
verse to reflect this.

Folk

8

Play a reel or two, or maybe three or four
Sound creation of a kind like nothing heard
before
Twanging of the banjo strings, the throb of
double bass
Resonating through the soul as tempo gathers
pace

A voice honed to perfection, not easy to ignore
Alluring accents amplify the audience rapport
And lines which spin a yarn and words which
tell a tale
A wealth of talent waiting in the wings to be
unveiled

Animated fiddler, squeeze box connoisseur
True eclectic mixture of a musical liqueur
The faultless nimble fingers of the strummers
from the north
Oh glory be to folk on high from now and this
point forth

I enjoy folk music. The easy-to-sing-along-to
tunes, the stories in the lyrics. It simply makes
me happy. So this is my ode to folk music where
I have attempted to make the poem sounds as
upbeat and bouncy as folk music itself.

Angel

I look at you each and every day
With love and in such awe
I remember clearly
The day that you were born

You have grown from tiny seed
And flourished into child
Most of the time with temperament
So lovely, meek and mild

You have a charm all of your own
You truly make me laugh
I love watching you play and learn
And those fun times in the bath

I stare at you at times
When you are fast asleep
And think of all the memories
Of you I'll fondly keep

Each day to me it plainly seems
That you learn something new
And I love seeing what you see
From your simplistic view

At times it seems that birth day
Was a long time back from here
But the emotions of that special day
Are still so crystal clear

And every day from then till now
Proud moments never cease
You bring to me fun and affection,
Noise… and sometimes peace!

My bundle of joy, my angel
With your little hands and feet
I love you now and every day
You have made my life complete

I always feel pensive in Autumn… and every
word of the above (watching my girls grow up)
is true.

Public transport

You wait for a few minutes and then three mini
poems come along at once…!

These lovely priority convenient seats
Aren't for any Tom, Dick or Harry

Unless Tom is pregnant, Dick is a senior
And Harry can't move with ease
Don't sit here in the priority seats
If others need them please!

Nice shoes darlin'! Fab trainers mate!
For this time of day, I have to say you're looking
kinda great
And if I possessed such footwear, I'd show the
world for sure
And maybe I would think such shoes were too
good for the floor
But as much as I'm in awe of your well-dressed
wondrous feet
Would you mind just keeping them firmly off
the seat?

We know you can't wait
And don't want to be late
Plus a comfy seat's in your sight

But when we open the door
Please don't ignore
The passengers trying to alight

I have to say I do get myself irritated travelling
on public transport at this time of the year.
People's shoes are dirtier, manners often seem to
be left at home. These three little ditties
summarise my biggest public transport gripes.
Take heed!

Rock, paper, scissors

You are a rock
I love that you care
You're a safe haven
And you're always there

You can be paper
That's ever so thin
Vulnerable, fragile
But strong fight within

You wield scissors
But never breach trust
You only use them
When needs must

Intertwined
Through and through
Three different traits
But all parts of you

I adore games and love the simplicity of the
game 'rock, paper, scissors' but it made me
think of each aspect of each entity in more detail
and perhaps we all possess the qualities and
properties of these objects.

Fruit fool

Hello old fruit
Fruit is silly:

Seedy papaya
Rhubarbed wire

Gooseberried six feet under
Pineapple wonder

Chronicles of Banarnia
Limes that won't harm ya

Up the apples and pears
Tangeriney stairs

A damson in distress
Lemony cit-ress

Kiwis are jolly
Or sometimes melon-choly

Grape expectations
Of blackcurrency fluctuations

And a satsumo wrestler
An orange no lesser

A ripe mandarin
Playing his mangolin

Have some fruit
Kumquat may
Let's go round the mulberry bush
With cherries on top
Old fruit.

Absolutely and completely nonsensical because
sometimes they are just the days I have; days
where I can't think straight and even normal
things seem ridiculous.

Teddy

I'll wrap you up with Teddy; make sure you hold
him tight
Keep him close to you and he will keep you safe
all night

He'll protect you in the dark and watch you
while you sleep
Remaining in your arms until you've finished
counting sheep

His nose may be a little cold; his fur will keep
you snug
All you have to do for him is promise him a hug

I'll wrap you up with Teddy; make sure you hold
him tight
Keep him close to you and he will keep you safe
all night

Yes it's a poem about a teddy bear. Originally
written with children in mind, I'm not afraid to
admit I'm still a huge lover of my teddy bears
and I find them a comfort. My bears have seen
the worst and best of me over the years. Do not
underestimate the power of a bear!

Let me speak

Oh let me get a word in
Don't talk over my voice
Although I'm normally quiet
I like to have the choice
To be quiet if I wish
To speak if I must
Because when I do
My words are like gold dust

I'm definitely more of a listener than a speaker.
It's always annoyed me when people talk over
me when I do make the effort to say my piece. If
I have something to say I want people to listen!

A dog's life

To see things from a dog's perspective
Is surely no bad thing
A renewed enthusiasm every day
And the joy that this does bring

They've walked this route a thousand times
Yet embrace it, fit to burst
And enjoy this thousandth walk again
As if it were their first

Their food, a mix of brown, and brown
Served in the same old bowl
Is welcomed with so much delight
As if mealtimes make them whole

The best companion you could have
A canine never judges
Always there; forever loyal
And will never harbour grudges

They'll be your fun, your entertainment
Protection to the end
They'll try your patience too of course
But will always be your friend

They may chew shoes, your mail or worse!
You may question what you've smelt!
But these bundles of joy guarantee
Your heart will always melt

That heartening sense when you get home
A feeling you can't ignore
The 'pleased-to-see-you' and waggy tail
When you walk through the door

A stroke here, a cuddle there
That's all they really need
When the love's reciprocated
That's all and well indeed

Simplistic life, they don't ask much
As long as you're right there
No materialistic need
Just acknowledgement you care

In summary what I'm trying to say
In this closing epilogue
Is perhaps we should all strive to be
A little bit more 'dog'

We rescued a little scruffy brown mixed breed in
January 2023. Yes she's a little bit unpredictable

and a tad naughty but you cannot fault her in any
other way – she's a perfect companion. Why
can't people be more simplistic and more
'dog'?!

Land of nod

Think nice thoughts my little one; float to a
world of dreams
No problem in the land of nod's as big as first it
seems

There's no need to fret my dear, you are out of
harm's way
You just need to bear in mind tomorrow's a new
day

Another poem written with children in mind but
it is in fact can be comforting for all of us.

Walks

Take a deep breath; breathe in the view
For walking is a great thing to do

The views are different every day
Whether bright and sunny, dull or grey

The same routes differ as seasons change
As moon and sun their paths exchange

A knobbly stick, a cute green stalk
So much to see when out for a walk

Look more closely and you will see
Nature living, naturally

Autumnal colours; veiny leaves
Squirrelled nuts by furry thieves

A paw print medley; large and small
And other markings from those who crawl

Time to think, situations to ponder
Life is good when you take a wander

A floral scent, then hint of death
The fleeting dewy mist of breath

A frozen web, a soft white feather
The distant haze of purple heather

A flurry of colour, a wisp o' willo'
A hundred memories for tonight's pillow

Perfect for mind, body and soul
Life rights itself when taking a stroll

Anybody who knows me knows that I love my
walks. If I don't get out, I get tetchy. There is so
much to see out there, even if you walk the same
routes every day. And, in the Autumn, things get
especially beautiful.

The clutch

Like, unlike, comment, post
Whose is the status we love the most?

Tag, upload, share, don't poke
We learn so much about fellow folk

But is it real or is it fake?
It's hard to know what to make

News Feed, check-in everywhere
People must know we're here or there

Update profile, change our pic
Smirk at people getting stick

Tweet (or X post?) – selective or not
Are these friends – or should we block?

We're in the social media clutch
We need to log in way too much

Release me from the constant scroll
Give me back my life's control

I don't even think you can 'poke' on social media anymore although I liked the feeling of giving somebody a virtual poke! Just goes to show how quickly things change. Anyway, I love social media and dislike it in equal measure.

What I think about you

I adore pen and paper, words and rhyme
And when the urge takes me, I make time
To jot down feelings, thoughts and prayer
Some too private but some I'll share

When it comes to the love I feel for you
They're the best words I know, timesed by two
But I'm not sure I'm even close to expressing
And to fail at this task would be depressing

You are both my life; my happiness and laughter
Followed by joy, smiles and everything after
You have your quirks and trickiness
But even at these times I love you no less

You're beautiful, witty, intelligent, kind
You have compassion for others but know your
own mind
There are times when you want me when you
feel in a muddle
But nothing is in doubt after a fix-it-all cuddle

My love for my children knows no end
And I'm not even sure the words I've penned
Show the everlasting love that I impart
For both of my girls – deep in my heart

I know, I know – another 'thoughtful' one but I sometimes feel that my words to my children are not enough and perhaps, if they rhyme, it shows more thought has gone into it. I know they will read this one day and it will all make sense to them.

We're all different

Remember that everyone's different
Not everyone's like you or me
And let's face it for one moment
We wouldn't want them to be!

Scared of your own shadow
Amazingly self-possessed
Brave as brave can be
Down, worried, depressed

Kind, generous, sensitive
Arrogant, confident, brash
People-pleaser, genuine
Or a true desire to clash

A trait or personality comes
In its own shape and size
Some we warmly welcome
And some we deeply despise

Of some bits we're embarrassed
Of others we hold pride
Yet we can't really change
Who we are inside

To be ourself should be
Our only true life aim
Existence would be too sad
If we were all the same!

Gosh I am glad really that we're all different. If everyone was like me then goodness help the poor world!

My jigsaw pieces

You know how I am put together
You know what makes me tick
You know what I find complicated
You know what makes me sick

You know how I react to things
You know what makes me cross
You know when I'm contented
And when I'm at a loss

You know when I am thoughtful
Those times I'm reminiscing
You know of all my pieces
And when one of them is missing

You are very special if you recognise when a
friend has a missing piece…

A poem about a poem

Write a poem – twenty-one days
"Why not?" I think "That won't phase
Me. Easy to do – one per day
Nothing else to get in my way."

Parenting on hold, chores can halt
I must consult thoughts in the vault
Of my brain. Crumbs, content's light!
Very slim pickings on topics to write.

It's easy to craft when a subject is clear
If someone gives me that initial idea
But when I have to start from scratch
There's work to do; a plan to hatch.

I'm sure I can pen something in a short time
It's not as if it has to rhyme
I mean they don't have to – but if they do
I feel I've achieved a thing or two.

But what's annoying is when they won't scan
And I write and re-write as many ways as I can
Chopping and changing that word and this
And hoping the reader spots nothing amiss.

I hate to disappoint the poetry-lover
But I couldn't find a topic to cover
I wanted to raise at least a small smile
But I've pondered these words for quite a long
while.

Amazing alliteration to take on board
Trying to strike a colourful chord
Wanting to win my readers' respect
Spellcheck. Grammar. Carefully checked.

Metaphors and similes are good to include
But expert bookworms, advise how you'd
Fit one in this verse; along with the knack
Of writing well, as sharp as a tack?

How can I compare to a summer's day
When I really don't know what to say
After all I'd no great topic in mind
And started writing this pretty much blind

So I had nothing to write about this Autumn day
But I've scribed this poem anyway
A ditty about having nothing to write
I hope I sort of did alright.

Need I say more?! I literally ran out of topics so wrote a poem about not having anything to write about!

First day

Frightening but excited
Incredible big school
Rewarding golden tickets
Sit tall
Timetables to remember

Determined to learn new things
Answering questions
Yes, I can do this!

One thing I associate with this time of year is the whole 'back to school' thing. So I had to share this poem – the only one not written by me but in fact by my youngest about her first day at secondary school - in acrostic format. Very proud of her.